Aversive at threshold

Zein Amro

BookLeaf Publishing

India | USA | UK

Presentation by *BookLeaf Publishing*

Web: www.bookleafpub.com

E-mail: info@bookleafpub.com

ISBN: 9789357690942

First edition 2022

DEDICATION

I dedicate this book to all those who have influenced the pieces of my writing, although discretion is warranted here.

ACKNOWLEDGEMENT

I acknowledge my friend Ines Semendric for putting me on to this and challenging me.

PREFACE

I was sitting in the office talking with my friend Ines regarding my recent efforts to get back into poetry and that same afternoon, she sent me the advertisement for this. I am a firm believer in things happening at their given time (although I speculate her phone was just listening to our conversation as technology does nowadays). Nonetheless, that is how it started and this were I am now.

Foundation

It's hard to love,
when your foundation was cracked.

My hearts ink

My tears are an unlimited source of ink,
As I write, my eyes well up and I blink,
Bleeding down from my heart as my love takes form and
befriends gravity,
Pelleted on my sheet,
Like rain on a sunny day,
Random, fleeting and quick to dry,
Until it rains again, as for now,
My tear ducts dry and I face inwards and internally cry.

In my head

I'm a novice at realism,
But a master of imagination.

BCN

Grey scale,
Simple but bland,
Alone,
My comfort land,
Change,
A flight away,
Colored,
Here I wish to stay,
Hot,
The skin to the touch,
Cooled,
By my summers crush,
Time,
Dragged on for some,
For me,
Hours melted to one,
Worries,
Ceased to matter,
By your eyes,
In them scatter,
Parted,
On an average street,
Static,
My heart aches to beat,
Salt,
Tears run down my cheek,
A kiss,
I long to meet,
Simple,
Life was then,
10 days, my spanish reign,
Sat,
Aching for one,
Your touch beneath the Barcelona sun.

Detachment

Falling for you was not hard,
detaching from you was.

A winter boy

Sit, idle, within, and desaturate,
My beaten but steadfast soul,
Peaceful, in the abyss you will find comfort,
The abyss within it calls,
For I did stare too long into it, for it to look back at us,
But don't mind,
I sought it out,
The silence that betrothed the night,
And everything to reach it we sold,
Our version of beauty,
An eternal winter cold.

Luna

Habibi if I am the ocean,
You are the moon,
Depth I've got plenty,
But you alone govern my tides,
And, in them I swoon.

Brown eyes

In your eyes I melt like butter,
By your touch alone I stutter,
three words I begin to mutter,
words I have said to no other.

Dear me

My love you built walls,
And photos you avoided,
My love you roamed empty halls,
In your mind hate you anointed,
My love you stared at the mirror in void,
As shame and disgust consumed you,
My love all you destroyed,
Yet rebuilt it all from rubbles anew,
My love I am happy,
That you since began to love you the way I do,
And the reflection you once feared,
Does not split your heart in two.

It's ok, I know

It's ok, after all this time you need not speak now,
The silence spoke enough,
And in the silence you should remain.

Quick recall

The first I let go off but still lives in my heart,
The second I would marry but we live worlds apart,
the third... I hope lives close, that would be a healthy start.

Lessons

I am molded by my failures,
and, accessorized by my achievements.

Pot of greed

I fill my cup,
But I thirst for more,
So I look beyond,
For a little pour,
But to overfill,
Is to overlook,
And greed himself,
His hands I've shook,
For I ran too fast,
Without caution or care,
And from the sides,
My vessel could not fair.

All the best

I fill my glass with the tears of our past as I cheers for your new found future.

Year round

15

Loving me was seasonal,
Loving you was seasonless.

Passing thought

Everything I care for has left,
Maybe this time I'll care less.
... Who am I kidding.

Another romantic

The version in my head of you was better,
soft notes down a suburban street,
and to that version I will remain tethered,
on loop, synced to my hearts beat.

On another note: I love you mum

My mother stands tall like a lighthouse,
On a rough and rocky terrain,
And yet she has always guided me,
Provided light piercing the harshest of rain,
On a raft I set alone,
To grow, learn and to seek,
And behind I left her idle,
A farewell too hard to speak,
And yet no matter the journey,
The relentlessness of the sea,
My mother to all I owe to,
Has always illuminated where shore would be,
But I fear one day without warning,
This never dimmed light may fade,
And in the darkness you will find me,
Estranged, lost and afraid.

Atlantis

Don't swim or float,
Rather, sink and submerge,
Deeper and deeper within,
That is when the real you will emerge.

Coffee shop

Freshly poured, a perfect blend,
at a coffee shop, in the east end,
Tatted baristas, a catch up with friends,
Another, drafting a paper to send,
Must be the aroma of the coffee grind,
That fuels this students minute grind,
But in all this symphony, productivity I find,
So, I begin, In my ears Einaudi,
Now, this experience desaturates but another begins,
A minute ten in and my focus filters,
To three, my coffee, thesis and me.

Dear reader

I don't suffer from heartbreak although that may be what it
seems,
I suffer from memories,
The vividness of the dreams.

www.ingramcontent.com/pod-product-compliance
Lightning Source LLC
LaVergne TN
LVHW021357200726
843509LV00014B/2892